Financial Freedom with Real Estate Investing:

Think Like a Real Estate Agent and Learn About Wholesaling, Property Marketing and Sales for a Beginning Investor

Minerva Publishing Services & Company

Table of Contents

Introduction

We believe that a solid foundation and understanding is crucial in order to excel in any sort of investment. We want you to have accurate, up-to-date information on the subject.

This book is for a beginner that is looking to build a solid foundation on the concept of real estate investing. You should feel knowledgeable and empowered at the end of reading this book and know where to start and where to look when it comes to this type of investing.

Throughout this book, we will be providing you with a roadmap to acquiring the basic knowledge on real estate investing. We won't get into too many specific calculation examples or even fully explore all the costs that will come along, but we will identify them and create a nice checklist so you can feel confident when making your first investment.

There will be an emphasis on the kind of mindset an investor needs to succeed. Though you might have the money and connections, the wrong mindset can lead to poor decisions. We will give you the confidence needed to know what real estate investing even is and how you can get started as soon as the end of the day.

We will also identify the biggest roadblocks and mistakes that new investors, as well as seasoned veterans, make throughout the book. The more you understand the risks, the better prepared you can be.

We will start discussing how much time and money investments could make. Prices are dependent on where you live and what you want to invest in, but we will still lay out the amount you should think about when starting off this type of investment.

As you read through the book, you will start to see all that you can gain from real estate investment. In order to do that, we will help you find the resources and people you should keep in mind in order to find your success.

While there are roadblocks with real estate investing, you should still feel empowered knowing that you are taking the initiative to become informed and gather the right information.

Chapter 1: What to Expect

There are many reasons that a person might want to become a real estate investor. Perhaps you are tired of your old job, but you don't want to have to start over. Maybe you are sick of never making enough money, and you want a passive way to increase your yearly salary. Whatever the reason may be, you likely have some expectations and goals going into this process that involve gaining a greater life.

There benefits of real estate investing that might help persuade you to choose this path, and it can also be very beneficial when it comes to doing your taxes. There are benefits that investors receive based on their decision to use their money a certain way, and you can find more write-offs that help you get a greater return.

Going into it, you should expect to be as knowledgeable as possible. The biggest mistake investors make includes not knowing what they were doing. Some risks will have negative effects, but for the most part, not getting what you originally wanted is the result of having little knowledge about a large investment. Certain things you will only be able to learn by experience, but there is plenty of information that exists out there already, and you shouldn't wait to take advantage of it.

What Real Estate Investing Is

Real estate investing is, on the surface level, putting money into houses, properties, buildings, and any location that you can own. Real estate investing involves buying apartment buildings or maybe just a small condo. It can mean buying acres with the intention of building a super shopping plaza with apartments above, or you could simply wish to buy the apartment building you currently occupy. There are no strict rules on what it means to invest in real estate.

It is not something that brings you instant success. Though you might be able to one day own those ten acres of land that you intend to turn into a housing development, at first, there are likely going to be smaller investments. Even if you have business elsewhere and are starting with a large sum of money, your first step shouldn't involve putting it all in one place.

Whatever level of work you want to put into, it will be indicative of what you get in return. If you want nothing to do with the process and are going to only hire people to do things for you, your return might be less than if you decide to do it all independently, hands-on, and having control over the entire process.

History of Real Estate Investing

It is easy to see that real estate investing is important now. You can't turn on the TV without some channel airing a show about a house flipper or someone looking to make money from property. It is the future for many people that want to start their own businesses, and it is also something enjoyable that gives people their free time back. When did all this start, however?

Investing in real estate has been around as long as the purchasing and trading of land and property has existed. The emergence of capitalism dating back to the early nineteenth century put an emphasis on expansive financial growth. When there is a pressure to make as much money as possible in quicker and less difficult ways, people start to look for ways they can make money from the money they already have. Investing is the way to do this, and doing so with real estate is a surefire way that people can have the security that they'll be making their money back.

As the overall economic market fluctuates, so does the real estate market. When times are tough, that can actually be better for investors, as they are going to be able to buy property for cheaper than if things were going well in the market. This might be a more long-term investment, as you'd have to wait for that to fluctuate up, but it is something we have to consider and remember about the past of real estate investment and our overall perspective on real estate.

Getting Started with Real Estate Investing

Real estate investing is far different from regular purchasing of real estate, and that's important to remember throughout the book and throughout your business plan. Though you might have already purchased your family home, that was a much different purchase than what you will make with your real estate plans. Having knowledge about the buying and closing process is important, but what you will look for and the deals you'll be making are going to be a lot different from what you did with the "forever" home.

You want to make sure that you have at least 20 percent of the closing price as a down payment. Anything less can put you at risk for a higher loan that might not have as big of a return. Aside from that, you will need more money for emergencies. This is going to be the first thing that you are going to want to do—find your down payment. If you have no money in your account right now and your credit is terrible, you can still become a successful real estate investor. All it is going to take is the willpower to save your money, and the passion to keep exploring real estate so you can be as knowledgeable as possible. Look at the houses around you so that you can get an idea of the property value. If you want to invest in a $300,000 home, you are going to want over $50,000 just to spend on the down payment.

Make sure that you familiarize yourself with the laws and codes for the places that you are investing as well. Though you might only be purchasing a home in the next town over, there could be completely different rules on what you can do with that property or how you are going to make the actual purchases.

Expectations vs. Myths

We hear all the time about success stories for people that managed to become millionaires after initial investments. These kinds of stories give us an idea of what we should expect. We think that with the right property, we could go from having $10,000 in our bank account to $1,000,000 in a year. Maybe you will find that quick jump one day, but for most people, it is going to be a slower growth.

Remember that there are a lot of myths. While it can be helpful to learn the stories of others so that you can understand common mistakes, you have to realize that there are some myths and ideations about this process already in place. One of them is that success happens overnight. While it might only take a few days for a deal to go through, you are not going to become a millionaire on that first deal. If you are, it is because you were already very close to becoming a millionaire. Your growth will be slow at first, but eventually, you'll hit a place where the money is consistently coming in.

Another myth that we need to forget about is the idea that success is black and white—that you are either successful or you fail. There are going to be times when you make mistakes and invest in the wrong things. There will be other times that you thought a deal would go through, but it all falls through, and you lose out on time and money.

That doesn't mean you won't still find success. In fact, these more difficult times can help us learn from our mistakes and do better in the end.

Return on Investment

Knowing the return, you'll get on investments, as referred to as ROI, is important, especially when comparing where you should put your money. This is a measurement that can tell you the efficiency that an investment has. It will help you to determine what the amount that you will get in returns will be.

The basic formula involves taking the value of the investment (x) minus the cost of the investment (y), and then dividing that by the cost of the investment (y).

$$(x - y)/(y) = ROI$$

You will then get a decimal, and this is going to help you determine the percentage that you will be getting back. The higher the decimal, the better the investment.

You aren't always going to find success with comparisons of this method; however, as it will be a decimal, it is not a number that you can look at and see, you'll get $14,000 back from one investment and $17,000 from the other, making the second one seem better. Instead, it is comparing those numbers and telling you which one is going to be a bigger return based on what you are putting in initially.

Investors Mindset

In order to make sure that you are going to find success, you have to find the right mindset. You can have all the tools that you need to get started, but if your mind isn't prepared for what's to come, then you won't find as much success.

Make sure that you are prepared and coming up with a plan of action. The biggest mistake many new investors make is that they are completely unprepared. They will think that just because they have the money to spend, they can do no wrong. In order to make substantial money, you have to start to find ways that you can actually make money from what you put out there.

Don't let other people's stories define your own. You are going to have moments where you might lose some. Always remember that success is like a roller coaster, where you will have to go down some hills before you make it to the highest point.

Key Takeaways

- Investing has been around for a long time, and we can be certain that real estate investment will continue to be just as crucial. It is a beneficial way that many people can make money and find financial freedom.

- There are a lot of myths surrounding real estate investment. Though there is a lot to be learned in the mistakes of others, we have to remember that what someone else went through isn't the definition of what we have to do to find success.

- Though we're going to be giving helpful tools throughout the book, the most important thing you can have is the right mindset. This is what's going to help you really find the financial freedom you've been looking for.

Chapter 2: Financial Planning

You have to come up with a forefront before you think about buying a property. You might have a solid action plan, but if you don't have just as sturdy of a financial plan, then things can start to really fall apart. A backup plan is very important, especially when you first invest. You might have the loan and down payment to get started, but what if the return that you are expecting isn't there? Do you have enough money to wait for the market to increase and sell later, or will you be able to handle a potential loss?

Don't be surprised by the future—know your prices. The more familiar you can make yourself with the different prices on houses and properties, the better you will be able to negotiate.

To start your financial plan, create an overall goal. Do you want to make thousands of passive income a year? Are you just looking to supplement your income every month? This will determine what type of properties you should choose to invest in. After that, you'll want to make smaller goals that will help carry you there. The more you can plan, the less of a chance for a mistake to take place. At the same time, don't over plan, because investing can be flaky and isn't always static.

Credit Score Importance

Everyone has a credit score, but very few people see the purpose or use of this. As a real estate investor, it is going to be very important that your credit score is high. This is why you might need to wait and save some money before you get started as well. Your credit will be bad if you have a history of missed payments or a high ratio of debt used versus debt available. You can also have bad credit if you've never owned a credit card, taken out a loan, or leased a vehicle. In order to build your credit, start small with a low-limit credit card.

Your credit score is a number that lets lessors see how reliable you are with paying back debt. When it is high, they're more likely to give you a loan and less interest, having the assurance that you can pay them back. A low score makes it seem as though you aren't as good at borrowing.

If you have a high credit score, you are going to be able to negotiate limits, interest rates, and other factors on different amounts that you are borrowing. If your score is low, don't worry. You can increase it by paying off debt and increasing your credit limit (but not spending it) so that investors can see you are reliable.

Make Money Work for You

All of our lives, we've been thinking about work. Even as kindergartners, we learned the different jobs there are and all along that comes with living a financial life. Before we were ever able to make money on our own, we were spending it. Many people also had "businesses" when they were kids, selling lemonade or candy.

Now, it is time to financially plan to make your money work for you. Instead of counting hours and watching the second hand slowly move at work, you can determine ways to find your money make more money. It can be hard to save at first, but once you do, you will realize that you can make even more money with the savings that are just sitting in the bank. Investing is a way that you can get money from doing little but with the assurance that something like gambling or winning the lottery gives.

The more money you make, the more money that you'll start to make. You might only be able to afford one house to flip at a time, but as your money grows, so will your abilities to invest in multiple properties. Before you know it, you can start to flip houses, create vacation rentals, and find ways of turning your property into a money-making machine.

Members You Want on Your Team

When it comes to building your team, you are going to first want members, like real estate agents, contractors, investing mentors, and an insurance agent. You might want financial independence and freedom, but that doesn't always mean doing it on your own. Using these professionals, especially in the beginning, is going to ensure that you aren't making any mistakes.

A mentor can be very helpful when you first start out. Look at the people in your life or in your community that have the success you desire. More often than not, successful people will be willing to mentor others. Though you might be a newbie, there's still something you can offer them, and they can help you in return. They could even be investors themselves.

Have an attorney on your side as well. Even if you feel acquainted with the laws and property regulations in place in your desired investment location, having an attorney will ensure that you don't have to worry about missing anything in that branch.

Financial experts are going to be clearly important, such as a personal banker or financial advisor. The more help you can afford, the better off you will be in the beginning. You won't have to have these people around the entire time, but it will certainly help when making your first few investments.

A general contractor can be there to help you make sure you know what you are getting into in terms of renovations. If you plan to flip a house, having a contractor you know and trust is going to make the process a lot easier.

Real Estate Networking

Networking is important in any business world, but especially the world of real estate investing. You want to get in with the real estate agents in your area and become aware of those that are buying the most valuable properties. Though it might seem like a competitive market, there's room for everyone if you play your cards right.

Remember that you aren't someone who has to be reliant on others. You are just making sure you have the tools you need to find success. Having people you can rely on is going to be important.

There will be people that present themselves as an individual willing to help, but they could just as easily be finding ways to use you, only to move onto someone else that's new and getting started in the business.

You are looking to make the most money possible, as are many other people.

These individuals might just be the people that decide to take advantage of you and get more money than you need to pay because they can see you are new. While not everyone will do this, it is important to find people you trust so you know you are not getting taken advantage of.

Looking through Your Lenders Eyes

What you have to remember as someone that is initially going to borrow money is that others will need a reason to have to give you the money. They aren't just going to do it. What will they get in return? When you are asking for loans and looking for mortgages, always remember to put yourself in your lender's shoes.

You also have to be prepared for what might happen if they say no. If you don't handle rejection properly, then they are not going to want to work with you in the future. Being professional and humble is crucial in this business as you never want to burn a real estate bridge.

Make sure that you are not only looking through your lender's eyes but the eyes of everyone else on the team. This is how you are going to be able to find success within this business.

Key Takeaways

- Money is what you are trying to make here, so knowing what you are going to do with it in the first place is very important. If you aren't prepared with a financial plan, insurance, and backup, then you might find yourself actually losing money in the end.

- Your credibility as a borrower is important. This will include your credit score and your ability to prove that you're trustworthy with other individuals. If your credit score is low now, you can still work on it to help ensure you are getting the best negotiations possible later on.

- Having people you trust surround you in this process is going to be very important. You never want to put yourself in a position that you might get taken advantage of. The more you can build a solid team, the better prepared you'll be to make the challenging decisions.

Chapter 3: Where to Look

Finding bids and deals is going to be your main focus. Sometimes, knowing where to look can feel very overwhelming, however. You will have to know how to search for good properties and, most importantly, where to look.

You have to have an idea of what you want from your return before you start looking. If you're going to invest in properties that you can flip for families, residential areas are going to be better. If you would rather be a landlord for individuals in studio apartments, city areas and places with nightlife are going to be better. Determine how a certain property is going to be used so you can decide where your best locations will be.

Looking local is a point that a lot of people will feel comfortable with starting at. When you can stick close to home and invest in things that you are familiar with, you will be able to identify the risks more easily. You will have a better sense of the type of people that live in a certain area if you happen to live in that area as well. You will know what kind of people will be buying your property so that you can better adjust your investments to that.

Risks

Make yourself aware of all the things that could be risky when it comes to your investment. Could there be an underlying issue with the house, such as if another home in the area might have had lead paint or asbestos? Is the traffic from the highway making the property less desirable? Could no one with the amount of money it takes to purchase your flipped home want to live in the area that you bought it?

Never think "It is not a big deal" when it comes to real estate investing. If there is even the smallest red flag when you are looking into a property, explore that. Something that seems like a little snow pile could actually be an iceberg, so never underestimate what a signal could be.

Look at the past and look at the future. You don't want to invest in a place that has a history of high crime, especially if the future looks as if it will stay that way for the next few years. You won't want to invest in an area that everyone seems to be moving out of even if there are still barely any rental properties in that area.

Types of Rental Properties

Investing in something you are going to flip or sit on is going to be a lot different than investing in a rental property. If you're flipping a home, you're only going to have to deal with that during renovations and the sale. If you're renting a place, it could be something that you manage for the next few years or even the rest of your life! You'll want to remember this when deciding what kind of rental properties you're investing in.

One type of rental property is a single-family home. You could purchase a home, and instead of living in it or buying it to sellers, you could simply rent it to families. This is common for people that are looking to move out of their starter home. If you currently own a home that seems to be in a prosperous area yet you've outgrown the space, you could still consider buying a second home and leasing the first out. This would be a way to make passive income.

Middle-class apartments can also be a good investment. Lower-class apartments can be investments, too, but you have to consider the upkeep that a less valuable would have versus the one that's recently renovated.

Higher-quality properties are important as well and can be rented to higher-income families or listed as vacation rentals. You can purchase these rentals and furnish them yourself as well, charging higher fees.

With all rentals, there are always going to be risks as a landlord. You might have to evict a tenant at some point, and that can be challenging. You could also deal with a huge loss that is caused by a tenant. Whatever it is, always remember that renting means you're giving other people, usually strangers, partial responsibility over your investments.

Finding Rental Properties

Again, looking locally is going to be a good first option. This way, you have a feel for the people that are going to be buying homes in your area. If you overlook locally and instead go to places that you aren't familiar with, then you might find it harder to determine what kind of renter you're selling to.

After that, you are going to want to determine what kind of rental property you want before looking at the place, because this will certainly determine what you are going to be deciding. You wouldn't want to buy an apartment building on the beach in a high-traffic area if you expect to be investing in lower- or middle-class families. This would probably be better as a vacation rental. Look for places that are going to be desirable for the types of renters that you're aiming to hit.

Researching Your Location

First, never invest in a property that you have never been to. This seems like an obvious rule, but you'd be surprised at how many people will try to do this. Spend time there beyond just looking at the house. Stay there for a few days so you can get a sense of the traffic, vibe, and overall demographics of people that are living in the place you're thinking about investing in.

After the basic level of understanding, you'll have on the location, it is time to look at the financial aspects. What are the other houses going for in the area? Are there newer things popping up, like shopping centers or businesses that will drive up the property value? Look at the houses or rental spaces most similar to yours when determining what a good price would be.

When something seems like a good investment, you have to then start to make an analysis, figure out your ROI, and compare it to your other options.

Always give yourself multiple options so that you can be more confident with your final decision. If you don't explore all your options, then you won't be able to compare if you're actually making the right investment.

Understanding Market Value

Understanding the fair market value, which is also sometimes seen as FMV, is important not just for initial investments but for all people that are owning property. Market value isn't just going to be the price you pay or the asking price. There is no exact calculation to determine market value either. The most important thing to remember is that you need to look at all aspects about a property to find the true FMV.

Market value can be determined through real estate appraisals, as well as comparable sales within the area for the same type of home. You likely won't be able to determine the market value of your investment on your own and will need the help of an appraiser or real estate agent at first. Get a few different quotes for your first investment as well so you can see not only what your best option could be but also who your best potential team members could be.

Leverage Buying (Costs)

Leverage buying involves using another person's money, whether it is a personal or bank loan. It is the comparison between how much money you are borrowing versus how much money the property is actually worth. This is an important figure because it will let you know if your loaned amount and purchase price are worth it, determining if you're going to be making a successful return or not.

Higher leveraging means that you are trying to have a higher ROI. Leverage buying is so important because if you only use the money that you already have, you won't be able to take those investments as far as if you also use someone else's.

Appreciation of Property

Appreciation is how much a certain property might increase in overall value. This is something that usually happens naturally over time. As more communities become developed, the higher the appreciation of that property will be. The opposite happens to the home, however. The longer a house exists without renovations or updates, the more it will actually depreciate.

If you only hold on to your investments for shorter periods, however, and make the necessary upgrades, you don't have to worry as much about depreciation.

This can end up being the way that you make the most money.

Look at your investments and how there might be an appreciation of the overall value. A certain location might not be the greatest now, but it could be the hot spot in three years, the same time it might take to renovate an apartment complex. Though it's a longer investment, it could have massive returns that wouldn't be there if you invested in something smaller.

Estimating Cash Flow on Property

Cash flow is what is going to be left after all the other expenses are paid. This doesn't just mean the price that you paid for the house. Expenses are everything else, like renovation costs or what it took to pay off a certain loan. We will go over these expenses in chapter 5.

In order to make sure that you are getting a real estimate, you first have to identify everything that's going to cost you money. Perhaps the houses in an area are going for $200,000 newly renovated, and you found one that's $130,000 and needs serious renovations. That doesn't mean that right away you'll get $70,000 in cash flow. Your cash flow would be the likely $20,000 that's left over after closing costs, renovation, and realtor fees to sell the house again.

Cash flow can be an easy equation to determine. What you want to do is take the total income minus the total expenses. Determining your expenses is dependent completely on the property, but we'll go over what more you can start to expect in chapter 5.

Different Mindsets for Each Unique Home

You have to approach each new property with a different mindset. If you're selling condos on the coast of Florida and family homes in the middle of Ohio, these are two completely different types of properties. Though some processes are the same, buying, renovating, and selling are all going to be different.

What are your goals for the property? Though we all might have the simple goal of wanting to make more money, we can't have this be our only motivation from property to property.

Will there be someone that's living in the home, renting, or doing any more fixing up? Is the home something you're going to sit on for a few years, or are you trying to get it gone as fast as possible? Make sure that you are adjusting your mindset based on the property.

People to Be in Contact as Resources

Keep an appraiser around so that they can help you with different investments. The more people you can trust and have on your team, the more resources you have in making the right investments. Real estate agents, brokers, and contractors are all there as people that want to make money, too, so if you find ways to work together, you will only be able to help yourself out more than if you tried to do it all alone.

Key Takeaways

- Before you can decide where you want to buy a certain property, you have to determine what the use of that land is going to be. Is it a rental for students or a place for families to vacation?

- There are so many risks when it comes to investing, even still with real estate. You never want to underestimate a sign that something could be wrong, and don't let yourself ignore red flags. If it doesn't feel right, remember that you can always find a better investment that will fit better.

- No two properties are alike, so always remember the importance they all hold on an individual level.

Chapter 4: Investment Strategies

Not all investors do the same things in order to make money. If you look at the top investors of all time, they all likely have very different strategies. Some people will find success with rentals; others prefer flipping. You might want to use apps like Airbnb to make money, or perhaps you would rather buy property and sell it later as the value rises.

You have to look at what works best for you based on your (1) goals, (2) amount of money, and (3) the actual type of property.

Once you can determine these three things, you can then decide what strategy is going to bring you the most money. You don't have to use this strategy for every investment you make either. In fact, you should always try new investments as a way to diversify your portfolio and articulate your skills as a real estate investor.

Buy and Hold

Buying and holding is a term you might often hear when people are discussing stocks. This applies to investments that involve real estate as well. This is a more passive strategy and is good for those that have a lot of money and people that don't want to do that much work.

It will involve you owning property and holding on to it as the market fluctuates. It can be scary because you might buy a property and the value drops within a few months. It's important to be prepared for this, however, because in five, ten, or more years, it could double in value.

The hardest part about this strategy is knowing when to let go and when to make the sale. Obviously, you want to hold on to the property until it increases in value. This might never come, so there also has to be the acceptance that it was a faulty investment. You might also see the price start to rise, but you don't want to sell at this point either. When you can learn how to be patient and how to predict certain market fluctuations, you can master this method.

House Flipping

House flipping is becoming a popular way for many people to make money. It's a great way to establish a company in terms of branding and style and allows you to make a lot more money if you're willing to put in extra work.

Although it is popular, there are a lot of people that don't want to have to do the construction themselves. A lot of people have the fantasy of fixing up a house, but few people actually will, and many buyers just want something that is move-in ready.

This is when it is important to have a loyal contractor that's going to help you make sure you have all the money needed for the repairs. You can bring the contractor with you when hunting for a new investment to make sure that you are aware of everything that could go wrong or cost you more money in the end.

Student, Short-Term, and Vacation Rentals

Short-term rentals where there is going to be a lot of turnovers can help people make money. This is because renters will often have to pay higher amounts for shorter agreed-upon times. Think of it like a hotel. You might pay $100 a night to share a room with your coworker on a business vacation. At home, however, you pay $500 an entire month for a studio apartment with more space and privacy.

If you have a two-bedroom apartment, you could make $600 in monthly rent from a long-term tenant, or you could earn $600 a week by renting it out to vacationers. This is a great way to make more money, but there's a little more risk than with regular rentals.

The issue with this is there is going to be more risk and upkeep. You will have to likely pay for cleaning services if you're renting to vacationers. You might simply have to deal with some dramatic instances. Someone might not want to pay for their vacation because of a small reason that you had nothing to do with, or you might end up having people damage your property.

BRRRR Investing

BRRRR investing involves buying, rehabbing, renting, refinancing, and repeating. Buying is the first step, which involves the purchase of your desired property. Then you rehab that space only to rent it out. After a while, you can refinance the place and pay less for it while still making a passive income from the rent of your lessees. Then you can repeat the process and watch as your wealth grows.

This is a great method for many people to use as long as they're willing to put in the work. You will have to deal with both the process of renovations and what it's like to be a landlord that deals with renters.

This strategy also hits a few different things that are important as a real estate investor, however. You are making more money from a property because of the work in renovations you put in. You are also making passive income from renting, so it's a great way to make money in more ways than one.

Wholesaling

Wholesaling involves never actually owning a home. Instead, you are more like a middle man. As the whole seller, you would contract the home seller to agree upon a price, market that to buyers, and then give that contract to a potential buyer. You would make an estimate on the cost and value of a home, including the price of renovations. This is a great method for people that don't want to deal with the headache of all the buying and closing. However, you also need to make sure everything is still done legally and in writing to protect you and your money.

Key Takeaways

- There is more than one strategy you can choose when getting started with real estate investments. Your strategy is dependent on your personal goals and the type of property that you're expecting to invest in.

- Anything that involves renovations is going to be more time-consuming and harder work. However, it might end up giving you more of a quicker return as you don't have to wait for natural appreciation and are instead creating it yourself.

- Renting is a great way to make more money long-term, but it can be challenging as well. There are risks with renting, but it's still a great way to make passive income with little work compared to some investments.

Chapter 5: Buying and Closing on a Property

Now that you know the steps it takes to purchase a home, you are going to have to look deeper at the expenses and the other important information that some investors overlook when they first start out. You can see the asking price of a house simply for what it is, but that is only the main portion of what you're actually going to have to pay.

Once you have decided which property to purchase, it can be an exciting time. The thrill of the sale and knowing that you are investing in your future. All that anxiety over the purchase hasn't ended just yet as you still have to go through an inspection.

Closing can be just as stressful as the buying process for many investors and homeowners in general. Before closing, there is always a chance that the deal will still fall through. Remember that when investing. Also, consider the other finances we'll be discussing in this chapter.

Financing and Loans

You might be an investor going into this brand-new,

all on your own. Perhaps you know other investors that got you interested in the market. Whatever it is, you likely already have a method of financing that you are preparing. Perhaps it is a loan with others, or maybe you are financing it all on your own.

If you aren't sure what you want to do, there are still plenty of options for you. Cash financing is usually the easiest option because it is your own money that you don't have to worry about paying back. You can use a private money lender who is a knowledgeable investor looking for prospects like you to get started.

You could even have the option of seller financing, in which you and the seller strike up a deal. When you choose to do this, it is important to ensure that you are still getting the legal protection needed should something go wrong.

Mortgages

Mortgages are amounts borrowed used to purchase real estate in which the buyer is promised to pay back within a certain time frame with the real estate being collateral for the payment. Most mortgages are taken out through banks. If the mortgage payments are consistently missed and all other options were exhausted by the owner, then the bank can foreclose on a home, meaning that they are then the owners.

Mortgages are how people are able to afford houses because rarely can someone afford to buy a house outright. A person with a job that pays $50,000 a year would have to wait a decade to buy a $200,000 house, but with a mortgage, they just might be able to pay for it.

This is the avenue that people will most often take when purchasing a home, and it is something for you to consider. Your payments will be based on your income, credit score, and the amount of the house. The more expensive the house, the higher the mortgage. The worse your credit score, the higher your interest rates.

Fixed vs. Adjustable

A fixed loan is one in which the interest rate will not change as time goes on. This means if you start with a 10 percent APR, it stays that way even if the economy crashes or does astronomically better. Your interest rate will never change with a fixed loan.

When it is adjustable, it can be altered depending on time and a few other factors that might increase or decrease the interest amount. This means you might pay 1 percent interest in the first six months, then 5 percent in the next six, 10 percent after the first year, and a 3 percent increase each year until a maximum percentage is reached.

Adjustable rates will usually be initially lower than the rates of a fixed interest. You will often be able to know the interest rate that will be there in the future, but sometimes there might be a determining factor that raises it.

You should determine what's best for you based on the time that you will be owning that home. For example, if you're only going to be owning for three months, an adjustable loan with an interest rate of 5 percent would be better than a fixed loan at 5 percent. A fixed loan is usually better for those that are planning on holding on to their property for a while.

Real Estate Mortgage Broker

A mortgage broker is a way that you can find good options for financing your home. These people are experts in mortgages and know how to find the right one based on your needs.

You might pay for the broker, but they're often paid for by the lenders. This helps you have a useful resource that will ensure you're making the right investment and not one blindly based on the first thing that seemed to work.

This is going to be especially helpful depending on what kind of loan you are deciding to take, fixed or adjustable. A mortgage broker will find you deals that will work best for you and give you comparable rates so you can feel confident you're making the best choice.

Down Payment

It is a good rule of thumb to have at least 20 percent of a down payment for the investment property of your choice. Some people will say 15 percent, but in terms of investing, you always want more.

The more that you put down, the lower your interest rates will be. The lower your mortgages might be as well, which could be helpful if you're investing long-term.

More financial standards need to be considered when saving money for your investment property.

You want to have the money for the down payment, but there will be a lot of other hidden costs as well. You can expect that there will be fees, taxes, and insurance rates close to 3–10 percent of the market value on a home.

Your credit score and current financial standing could also affect what your payments might be. This is why it's important to make sure that you're not just someone with money but a person in a decent financial standing to make sure you can avoid paying unnecessarily high fees.

Types of Costs

First, you have to think of the cost of a house, and then you have to look at what you are going to be getting back. When you see that amount, you have to know it is actually going to end up being less than that because of all the costs that go into a home.

Of course, if you are renovating the homes, there will be a much higher cost. Even when you're considering renovations, don't forget other hidden fees beyond basic construction and furnishing. You might need to pay for more inspectors, and perhaps you have to get something re-zoned or pay a higher tax fee.

If you won't be renovating, there's still fees and other types of finances that you have to consider. We'll go over some of them in the next few sections, but remember that these aren't all the fees that you'll be experiencing.

Property Tax

Property taxes are yearly fees that we have to pay based on our home's value and location. Value is determined by the home's size, age, and renovations. Adding a room might increase the value of a home. At the same time, demolishing an old building could also increase property value. Location is simply where your property is. A lot close to the beach in California is going to have higher taxes than a lot of the same size in middle-of-nowhere Iowa.

Make sure you look into how exactly your property taxes will be calculated but understand that there are very few similar things all investments will qualify for. Your property taxes are going to be calculated by not only the land but also the buildings that are on that land as well.

Inspection Fees

Inspections are necessary in order for a house to close. When the house is in escrow, this is when inspectors are usually called to come and look at the house. They will check for structure, infestation, and anything in the building that is not up to code. This is why it can be helpful if you have an inspector on your team when looking at homes, though they can't conduct official inspections until the house is in escrow.

You have to make sure that you are prepared to pay for this inspection. They are typically around $200–$400, depending on the location and size of the home. The inspectors are paid by the buyers. If you're making a very large investment over six digits, you might want to consider more than one inspector to make sure nothing is overlooked. Running into unexpected costs during renovation can be what really sets you back and puts you over budget.

Aside from the inspection fees, be prepared to pay for anything that might need to be fixed in the inspection. Perhaps a beam needs to be relocated or a pool needs filled in. You might work this into your deal with the seller as well should there be anything especially financially heavy.

Loan Costs

In addition to having to pay back the money that you are borrowing for a certain investment, you'll also be responsible for paying any fees and interest acquired throughout as well.

Loan costs will be less the less you borrow, and the better your credit history is.

You also have to consider closing costs on whatever your borrowed agreement is.

This includes any fees for acquiring documents, such as the application or your credit history. There will be insurance premiums, various inspections, taxes, and many other hidden fees that you can't overlook. You should be prepared to pay anywhere from 2 percent to 6 percent of the initial purchase price when it comes to closing costs.

Insurance Title

Since you are making an investment, there is going to be some risk involved. You'll have to make sure that you are prepared to pay title insurance to protect the lender. This is a way to secure their faith in you and protect them from losses acquired.

Though it protects the lender, you'll still be responsible for purchasing it. They might also require that you purchase an owner's insurance for yourself.

Negotiating Skills

There are a lot of different costs and fees, so it will be up to you to negotiate your best prices. While some people will have fixed prices, there will be a lot of negotiation involved in this kind of investing. The better you are at looking for good deals and convincing others to buy into these, the more money you will make in the end.

Don't say yes the first time. Let your investments get out there a little bit. If you say yes right away, it gives the buyer the idea that they could have bid lower and vice versa.

Be a cooperative person. No one will like to invest with you if it is difficult. The more you can network and build meaningful relationships in this business, the better off you will be in the long run.

Stand up for what you think is right. It will let people know that you are not going to settle for anything less than what you know you deserve.

Key Takeaways

- You don't have to have the entire sum of your initial investment. There are many different loans and mortgages you can take out, and using a broker to help you find a good one is a great option for beginners.

- There are a lot of fees that can be overlooked by real estate investors. Always remember to save extra money for costs that you might have forgotten about. Being unprepared with how much money this can actually take is a big flaw of some real estate investors.

- The better you are at negotiating, the more money you will save. Refine your skills to negotiate and practice deals and bidding so that you can put your best foot forward when starting off.

Chapter 6: While Owning

Once you finish the deal and get to a point where you are now a property owner, the work doesn't stop. Now, instead of a prospective buyer, you are on the other end as a property owner.

Don't wait around to get started with your next step as an owner. It can be very easy to get lost in projects. Keep up that same drive that led you to the purchase in the first place so you can stay on track with your goals and get your property sold ASAP.

If you are going to be holding on to the property for longer, then it is going to be important that you know what it means to be a landlord or lessor to the people that will be renting your home.

Upkeep

If you are keeping up a rented property, then upkeep is going to be very important. This is going to include all the maintenance involved in making sure that a property doesn't depreciate. You can do this yourself, or you can hire a team responsible for maintenance.

If you want to own a rental property for the next few decades, you have to be ready for larger costs like reroofing, replacing appliances, fixing the plumbing. There will be some long-term costs that can be covered by monthly rent of tenants, but there might be some things you just have to do out of pocket.

Remember that other people will be responsible for some upkeep, like keeping the floors clean and the garbage picked up, and that might not even happen. If renting to people with pets, that can cause property destruction as well. Though you will want to cover this before they move in through move-in fees or deposits, it can still be costly and time-consuming to fix up the damage other renters might have done.

Doing Inspections

Though you did some initial inspections to determine property value and to see whether the house was in good shape, you'd still have to do them as a homeowner. If you want to do inspections while someone else is living there, then it is going to be up to you to make sure that is written and agreed upon, as renters have their rights as well.

If you are going to be investing in vacation, then you

might consider having an inspection or cleaning fee to make sure that people will keep the place in good shape.

Adding Value to Property

It can be expensive to upgrade a home, but if you let it sit and make no changes, that can have just as much of a negative dent on your finances.

Adding value can simply be different cosmetic things. You might want to knock down a wall in a home or paint the outside a different color. Though you can get big returns from doing gut rehabs, you can also find your money working for itself when you make a few simple changes that increase the desire for a certain property.

Avoid getting too personal with the touches that you add. You want to look at every decision as one for the future of the home, not just based on the things that you already enjoy.

Rolling over Rental Property Profits

You might get to a point in your rental journey where you decide that you want to roll over your rental property profits into another real estate investment. The IRS identifies any attempt as an investment as such.

To do this, you might want to use a 1031 tax-free exchange, which will help when filling out your yearly returns. This is also known as a Starker Trust. It will help so you can defer these taxes rather than have to pay on the capital gains made during the initial investment.

REITs

REIT stands for real estate investment trusts. A REIT is a company in which ownership is obtained over real estate that is producing income. There are different requirements that a company has to meet in order to be considered a REIT.

These companies are beneficial to real estate investments because they give all investors the chance to make real money from their purchases. A REIT company will help provide competitive returns based on dividend income as well as capital appreciation.

Selling Real Estate

Once you've gone through all the steps of initially hunting, buying, and closing, it is time now to move on to the part where you make a sale that leads to a return.

The best way to make a good sale is to use a real estate agent as they will help to get you the highest price since they will get a high return as well.

Ensure that you are making the most from your home. If you are investing in multiple places at a time, it will be easier for you to decide longer term when to sell and if you should stay invested.

Key Takeaways

- The work doesn't stop once you've made the purchase! As a property owner, you have to consider short-term and long-term upkeep that you might need to do on a rented property.

- Don't look at selling as the only way to make money. You can roll over investments, or you can increase property value altogether, leading to higher rental rates.

Chapter 7: Financial Independence and Freedom

It will be hard at first. Eventually, however, you will find that you can actually gain financial independence from real estate investing. If you decide to flip houses and buy and sell rapidly, then you will see that each sale you make gets bigger and bigger. On the other hand, you can also decide to keep properties and add more, only increasing how much money you are making monthly.

Fund Your Future

Each time you reach a goal, look at it as the starting point for a new one. Reach further to fund your future. Look for innovative ways that you can grow your investments. No matter how much money you're making, remember that there is always room for improvement. While it is important to secure yourself for the future, make sure that you are still allowing this increase in wealth as a chance to take some risks. You won't want to be too risky in the beginning, but as time goes on, you will find it's easier to make more challenging decisions.

Putting It All Together

It is important to branch out and try new things. Diversification is going to allow a growing portfolio that will only advance your future attempts at real estate investing. At the end of the day, put it all together and look for ways that one growth opportunity can help another.

Remember that time is going to be the biggest aid in your investment journey.

Conclusion

Now, it is time for you to get started. You might be asking, "Where do I get started?" The very first thing that you should do is determine what your goal is. Secondly, you will have to look at how much you are realistically going to be able to invest. After that, determine what type of rental property you are looking for.

Action Plan

Once you have determined what exactly it is that you are looking for, it is time to find the property that's going to help you achieve your dreams. This can be done through a professional or on your own at first.

Next in your action plan should be the ways that you are going to secure your financing.

The final step is the buying and selling part. It will be up to you to determine if in between these two things, you are making adjustments and upgrades that will help the house sell better.

Effectiveness and Efficiency

Make sure that you are getting the most out of your investment. Effectiveness will be how likely you are to be making the money that you wanted in the first place. Efficiency is about how much of a certain rental property can be used to make money.

This is the last mistake that many investors will make. They think once they've purchased and closed on a home, it's time to move on. Don't be afraid to get creative and look outside the box for other ways to get your money to work for you.

References

"2019 Real Estate Forecast: What Home Buyers, Sellers and Investors Can Expect" (2019).

"8 Resources for Successful Real Estate Investing" (2019).

"Real Estate Investing: Finding Gold Takes Work and a Plan" (2019).

www.ingramcontent.com/pod-product-compliance
Lightning Source LLC
Chambersburg PA
CBHW070431180526
45158CB00017B/977